A gift for Joyce,
The Eyes of a child
Behold the wonder
of our
World.
With appreciation
Lisa R Cohen

Grace is Born

Copyright © 2013 by Lisa Rachel Cohen

ISBN: 978-0-9969010-1-7 (paperback)
Published in 2016 by Sparkle Press, LLC
2nd edition

First published in 2015 by Sparkle Press, LLC
ISBN 978-0-9969010-0-0 (paperback)

Inspired by my daughter *Alia*,

the song of my heart.

Grace is born

Written by Lisa R. Cohen

Illustrated by Judith Joseph

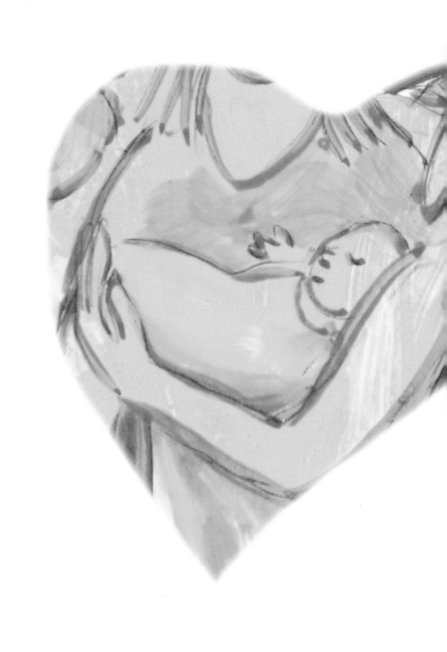

Grace is born.

Our Creator whispers into Grace her first breath,
"You are bathed in eternal light."

Grace exhales *hope*.

"Many will come to join you along the way."

Grace exhales *gratitude*.

*"Others will appear to question you
each and every day."*

Grace exhales *faith*.

Grace listens with a gentle heart

while searching for a place to start.

The sensation of creation *inspires* her to sing,
awakening in her the joy / her voice will bring.

Grace mingles and jingles

with those from all around,

noting frown after frown turning upside down.

Grace fine-tunes her *voice* over the years

to be worthy of magnificent cheer.

The voice of Grace

becomes the rave,

as melodies

flood from the stage.

Boys and men step in time,

joining girls and women

to chime the sublime.

The sound of delight *takes flight*.

All present are lifted in song,

Elated ...

Elevated

to where they belong.

Grace is placed on a pedestal,

deemed

the *singing angel.*

Grace catches her breath,

relinquishing her crown,

as Hope helps her down.

Grace explains,
"I am you,
you are me,
together
we create *harmony*."

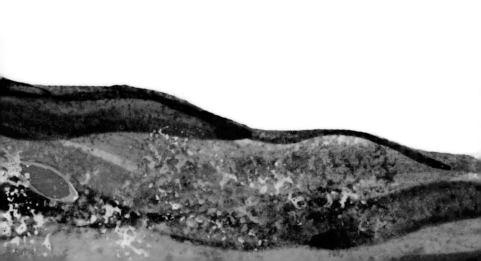

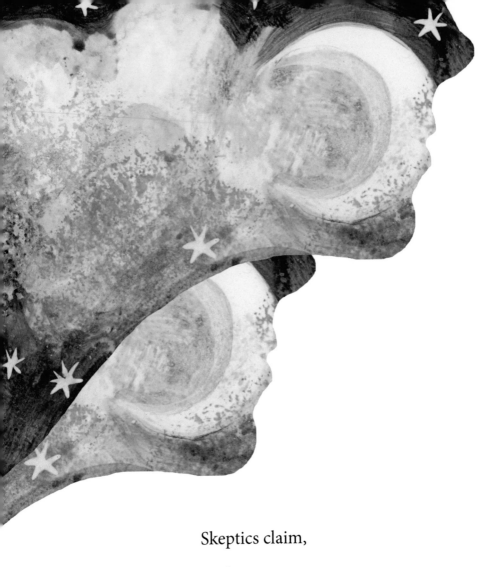

Skeptics claim,

"Grace is

a sham."

They search for smoke, mirrors

and the big shazam!

Cynics rumor,

"Grace was heard to gloat

that she could *heal*

with a single note."

Doubters demand to know

the secret to her success,

since Grace is undeniably different from the rest.

An unexpected audience arrives one day

when Grace and her ensemble

arrange to play.

Sensing an antagonistic air,

the crew warns Grace to

Be aware.

When the opening act

is ready to begin,

Grace becomes frightened

by the disturbing din.

The crowd chants,

"We want a cure!

That's what we came for."

Though expectations are unrealistic,

Grace prays to remain *optimistic*.

Grace invites them
to *sing* their song.

Reactions are startling and strong.

They rant:

"*Nobody cares.*

The rhythms of life

are too much to bear!"

Grace suggests they clap to the beat.

People *rise* in rebellion

and stomp their feet.

They demand:

"Make us feel better right away!"

They threaten:

"If you don't, there'll be a price to pay."

Grace inquires,

"What of their fate?"

urging them to participate.

They *fuse* together with fury.

Disharmony and dissonance amplify hate.

Violence and chaos escalate.

Grace embraces *Hope*

and waits with *Patience*

for *Faith* to arrive.

Grace exclaims,

"I can see

the light within

each and every one of you.

I feel your pain, know your disdain.

I hear your despair.

You have endured more than your share.

A disproportionate amount,

with losses too many to count.

I don't know why . . . "

With each tear,

the message becomes clear.

"You have lost your way,

been led astray

into the maze of madness,

wandering from end to end,

only to find yourself beginning again."

Halt!

"The Guardians of Light have been sent for you.

They are here

to dance with you throughout the night,

toward the source of *infinite* love and insight.

Look for sages of all ages,

wearing the face of every race,

talking the tongue of every one.

Listen for the Symphony of Divinity.

They will explain,

it is not here

you are meant to remain.

Should you resist,

they will insist

that within these walls of darkness,

life ceases to exist.

Open your heart

and

let the light in.

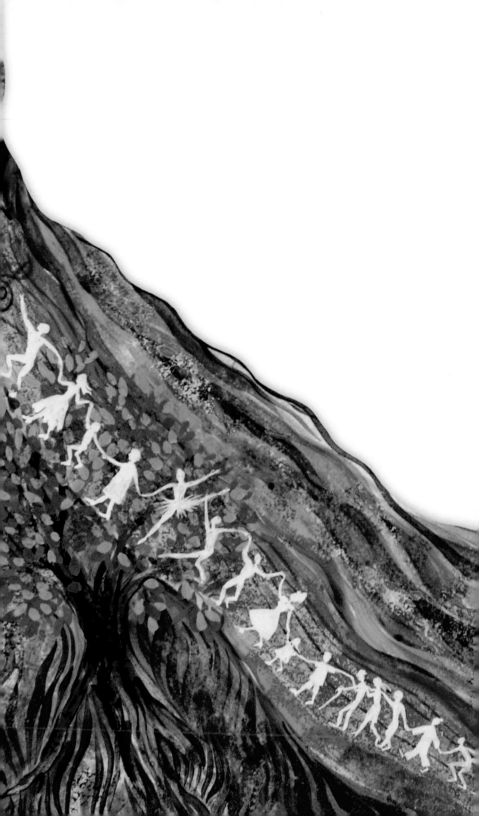

Take their hands.

Together you will far surpass the stance of survival

and become enraptured in the dance of revival."

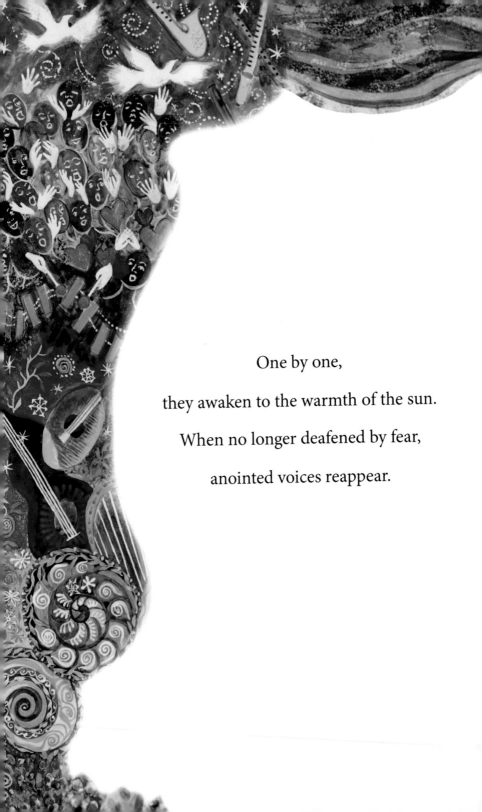

One by one,

they awaken to the warmth of the sun.

When no longer deafened by fear,

anointed voices reappear.

"Lessons and practice *expand* our range,

preparing us to become

instruments of change.

Lyrics of Love come from within and above.

So
reach out and up

and
fill your cup

with

Grace,

Hope

and

Faith

in each other."

Amen

In loving memory of my healing mentors

Rheva Cook

and

Bruce Burd

Your presence forever remains embraced by Grace

With Gratitude ...

To you,
for Illuminating and InSparkling our world with Loving Acts of Compassion

*With lavish thanks
to my creative collaborators...*

Judith Joseph, fine artist, for your magnificent painting of Grace

Lisa Kaczar, for your brilliant cover and interior book design,
as well as your enthusiasm and expansive eye for color, composition and texture

Ruth H. Cohen, Arlene Olster and Ethan Simon, for your discerning
editorial services

Christina Daniels, AdaGeo Communications, LLC, for embracing *Grace is Born*
with faith, hope and enthusiasm

Lesha and Eric Moore, for your fine art photography

Maxine Wolf, for your faithful friendship and professional guidance

Selena Ashley Wong, Yvette Autin Warren, Risa Batterman Dera, Tonnella Bell,
Hugh Carberry, Jodi Chapman, Jay Chaskes, Marvin Chodes, Tammi Davis,
Donna Driscoll, Beth Dunoff, Sharla Feldscher, Shanna Forlano, Abby Freeburn,
Ramona Frye, Lisa Goetz, Sheila Grant, Rebecca Gruber, Karen Hasher, Gerry Henry,
Claudia Herman, Andrea Hoffman, Kathy Italiano, Melanie Jamerson Rock,
Brenda Lee Watson, Lori Levin, Lisa Mascieri, Helen McKenna,
Ameesha Mehta-Sampath, Randa Michel, Marissa Pei, Ashley Peter, Jennifer Poff,
Joyce Poff, Barbara Richter-Kobrin, Amy Rossano, Jennifer Rothstein,
Robin Rubin, Gail Saul, Howard Saul, Dorothy Saynisch, Rochel Serebryanski,
Karen Trager, Jennifer Warner, Marsha Weinstein, Nora Wheeler, Maylee Wolf
and April Yamasaki for your insightful assistance and affirming presence

To all those who I have had the honor of providing Speech-Language and Cognitive
Therapy services to throughout the years. You have taught me how to love and be loved
and I will continue to hold you and your families in my heart.

To the Mishnoon Film Productions' Crew, Bobbie Ragsdale and our Austin Soul Sisters

Traci Rosenberg, for your intuitive wisdom

Thank you, dear Creator, for

My loving Parents, Sondra & Sheldon
My devoted Husband, Scott
Our beloved Daughter, Alia
and our spirited Irish Setter, Cholly

I am infused with hope.

~ Lisa R. Cohen

Notes...